SOMETIMES I'M SAD

Visit our website at www.skyponypress.com.

10 9 8 7 6 5 4 3 2 1

Manufactured in China, June 2022
This product conforms to CPSIA 2008

Library of Congress Cataloging-in-Publication Data is available on file.

Text by Poppy O'Neill
Interior and cover design by Summersdale Publishers Ltd.
US edition editor: Nicole Frail

Print ISBN: 978-1-5107-7273-1

Printed in China

SOMETIMES I'M SAD

A Child's Guide to Positive and Negative Thoughts and Feelings

Poppy O'Neill
Foreword by Amanda Ashman-Wymbs

Sky Pony Press
New York

CONTENTS

FOREWORD

*Amanda Ashman-Wymbs, counselor and psychotherapist,
registered and accredited by the British Association
for Counseling and Psychotherapy*

Having worked in schools and the private sector with children and young people for many years, I have seen firsthand the difference that establishing and maintaining a positive mindset can make to well-being and mental health. Developing this in childhood sets a foundation for future happiness and good habits of perception and mind.

Sometimes I'm Sad is a superb guide and self-help workbook, which I highly recommend to help children work on a more positive and healthy relationship with themselves, others, and their environment. The book is laid out so that their journey is accompanied by a friendly monster named Chip, and gives clear and easy-to-understand instructions. It offers fun ways to help children to see and respect the good things in themselves and others, and to develop gratitude for what they have and who they are. It also places emphasis on helping them know and accept that the way they are, feel, and think is totally okay, too. It is packed with positive affirmations, exercises, and insightful emotional and psychological truths, and it has a friendly, simple, and attractive format that will help children reframe their mindset in enjoyable and practical ways. It offers a holistic approach to assisting a child in feeling good, including information and activities on food and exercise, helping the child understand the importance of keeping well physically as well as emotionally and mentally.

By working through this book, children will learn to accept themselves fully and grow in understanding while developing good mental habits that will influence them for the rest of their lives.

INTRODUCTION: A GUIDE FOR PARENTS AND CAREGIVERS

Sometimes I'm Sad is a guide for children who want to view themselves and the world in a more optimistic light. Using ideas, techniques, and activities inspired by the work of child psychologists, it will help your child understand that they can break free from negative thinking.

The word "positivity" is often used to gloss over difficult emotions and experiences, encouraging us to ignore feelings like sadness or anger in favor of happiness and gratitude. There's nothing wrong with negative thoughts and feelings; they're an essential part of life at any age. Hiding these emotions doesn't make them go away, and it also makes it more difficult for a child to communicate with adults when something is wrong.

That said, certain ways of expressing negative emotions can be harmful. So this book focuses on finding a balance between positivity and negativity, and expressing emotions in healthy ways.

Perhaps your child is quite pessimistic, and always seems to be disappointed in themselves or others. Or maybe they've had a difficult experience and are finding it hard to see the world in a positive way again.

This book is aimed at children ages 8 to 12, an age when awareness of social relationships increases and kids start to compare themselves with others and care about what their peers think of them. Coupled with the first signs of puberty and increasing pressures at school, it's no wonder this is a time when many kids struggle with negative feelings. If this sounds like your child, you're not alone. With your support, patience, and acceptance, your child can learn to find more joy in life, helping them grow into a confident, positive young person.

Signs of negative thinking in children

Every child is different, but these are some common indicators that your child is feeling down about life and could do with some support:

- They are reluctant to try new things

- They put themselves down

- They rarely show enthusiasm

- They seem disappointed in themselves and others, no matter what

- They give up if something is challenging

- They have very high expectations of themselves

- They criticize their appearance and abilities, and those of others

- They seem quick to anger

- They struggle to make friends

It can be useful to keep track of your child's negative (and positive) comments and behaviors in a journal. Remember: a certain amount of negativity is healthy and normal, so it's about getting a good balance.

It can be challenging to look closely at your child's mental and emotional health—sometimes we, as parents and caregivers, identify ways our children take after us, and this can be very uncomfortable. Be kind to yourself. You are giving your child an amazing gift by taking an interest in their well-being. We can all find a positive outlook, even when it feels difficult. Like a small flame, with patience and attention, it will grow.

How to use this book: For parents and caregivers

This book is for your child, so it's a good idea to let them take the lead. Show plenty of interest so they know you're ready to help or talk about any of the things they read here. Some children might be happy to work through the activities by themselves, while others will need more guidance and support.

Let them go at their own pace, and even if your child's pretty independent in that respect, you can still look through the book together and start a conversation about positive mental health and emotions. Let them know that you're interested and they can come to you with anything they've learned or realized, as well as to discuss any parts they've found helpful, unhelpful, challenging, or worthy of a closer look. One small way you can encourage positivity is to listen to their honest feedback on a book you've given them— ask them for both positives and negatives.

The activities are designed to get your child thinking about their thoughts and emotions; it's important for them to understand that they are the experts on how they think and feel, so there are no wrong answers. Hopefully, this book will help you and your child understand each other a little better, as well as to learn about how a positive outlook can enhance their view of the world and their place within it. Ultimately, the aim is to make them more resilient and able to enjoy life more. Naturally, if you have any concerns about your child's mental health, your doctor is the best person to go to for advice.

HOW TO USE THIS BOOK:
A GUIDE FOR CHILDREN

This book is for you if you often . . .

- Feel unhappy about yourself

- Speak unkindly about yourself

- Worry about showing your emotions

- Find it difficult to talk about your feelings

- Tend to think the worst will happen

- Worry about trying new things in case they don't go to plan

If that sounds like you—some of the time, or maybe a lot of the time—this book, bursting with activities and ideas, will help you understand your emotions, be kinder to yourself, and feel more positive.

There's no rush, so you can go as quickly or slowly through the book as you like. If you get stuck or want to talk about anything you read, you can ask a trusted adult to help, or just to listen. A trusted grown-up might be your parent, your caregiver, one of your teachers, another member of your family, or any adult you know well and feel comfortable talking to.

INTRODUCING CHIP THE MONSTER

Hi! I'm Chip, and I'm here to guide you through this book.
You'll see me on lots of the pages. I'm really looking forward
to showing you around. Are you ready? Let's go!

PART I: POSITIVITY AND ME

Are you ready to be positively you? In this chapter, we're going to learn all about you, and then we'll find out what positivity means, why it's important, and how it can help you feel calmer and happier.

ACTIVITY: ALL ABOUT ME!

Can you fill in each box so Chip can get to know you better? It's okay to leave one blank if you get stuck.

My name is . . .

I am __ years old.

I live with . . .

I'm really good at . . .

Three words that best describe me are . . .

ACTIVITY: MY LEAST FAVORITE THINGS

What things don't you like so much? Complete the sentences below.

*My least favorite subject at school is*_____.

*The worst food is*_____.

I think _____ *is boring.*

*I feel sad when*_____.

*I feel angry when*_____.

ACTIVITY: MY FAVORITE THINGS

Now let's think of the things you like the most.

My favorite thing to do is_____.

My favorite thing about me is_____.

My favorite toy is_____.

My favorite animal is_____.

My favorite book is_____.

I BELIEVE
IN MYSELF

HOW TO SPOT POSITIVITY AND NEGATIVITY

Positivity and negativity are pretty easy to spot, as long as you know the clues. Can you notice them in yourself and other people?

Being positive means finding something to be happy about and hoping for good things, even if you're having a bad day or feeling a difficult emotion.

Positivity clues

- Seeing interesting things everywhere

- Asking questions to learn more

- Being friendly and encouraging to others

- Standing up for yourself and others

- Talking kindly about others when they're not there

- If something goes wrong, trying again

Negativity is the opposite; it means thinking that things will get worse or go wrong, and finding something to get cross about, even if your day's going pretty well.

Negativity clues

- Seeing sad or disappointing things everywhere

- Using words like "always" and "never"

- Talking unkindly about others when they're not there

- Being rude when someone has tried hard

- Trying to make others feel bad about themselves

- Giving up when something small goes wrong

> **It's okay for someone else to say negative things, and it doesn't mean that you need to feel negative, too.**

> **Some days you might be feeling negative emotions and, when that happens, you don't need to pretend to feel happy or calm—no matter what anybody else says.**

It's impossible to be positive all the time, so there's no need to try! You don't need to hide your feelings just because they aren't hopeful or positive. Some days are really hard, and it's okay to feel negative.

SPREADING POSITIVITY (AND NEGATIVITY)

When someone is feeling negative, they might try to make others feel bad. Why is that?

Our brains love to fit in with others: it reminds us that we belong and have plenty of friends and family around. So if you're feeling bad about yourself, your brain will feel most comfy if those you're with feel bad about themselves, too. You might do this by being rude about someone else's work.

It's the same with positivity. If you're feeling happy and excited, your brain wants everyone to feel that way, so you might share your happiness by showing kindness.

ACTIVITY:
POSITIVITY QUIZ

Take this multiple-choice quiz to see how positive you are!

1. You feel upset about going to school—one of your friends is being unkind. What do you do?

a. Pretend not to notice your friend's unkind words

b. Let your friend know that they've upset you

c. Pretend to be ill so you don't have to go to school

2. You've made a mistake on your art homework. What do you do?

a. Blame someone else for the mistake

b. Find a way to make the mistake part of the picture

c. Screw up the picture and throw it in the bin

3. You've been feeling down all weekend. What do you do?

a. Smile, so no one can tell you're sad

b. Talk about it with your grown-up

c. Decide that you'll feel sad forever now

4. You have a brilliant idea in class. What do you do?

a. Keep it to yourself, so no one copies it

b. Put your hand up and share your idea with the class

c. Stay quiet—what if no one else thinks it's a good idea?

5. Your friend is feeling really worried about getting a new teacher. What do you do?

a. Tell your friend to stop worrying and think happy thoughts

b. Listen to your friend talk about their worries

c. Tell your friend all the things that you're worried about right now

Mostly A: You worry about what other people think of you, and you don't let your true feelings show, in case they upset someone else. It's great that you care so much about others, but it's important to remember that it's okay to feel negative and make mistakes.

Mostly B: You're a pretty positive person. You respect yourself and others, even when it's tricky.

Mostly C: The world can be a scary and sad place sometimes. It's important to look for the good things, so you can feel positive feelings, too.

ACTIVITY:
WHAT I'D LIKE TO PUT IN THE TRASH

Chip doesn't like competitions. They make Chip feel worried and the feeling of losing is really horrible. Chip wishes all competitions would just get in the trash!

It's okay if there are things you don't like. Everyone has different likes and dislikes; we don't have to agree—that's what makes life so interesting. Being honest about the things you don't like helps you enjoy the things you *do* like more. Even though we can't really put these things in the trash (unless you've drawn banana skins!), it can feel good to imagine what it would be like if we could.

What would you like to put in the trash? Draw or write it here:

ALL EMOTIONS ARE OKAY

Emotions are a big part of being human. Imagine how boring life would be if you never felt excited, or nervous, or angry?

Emotions are our bodies' way of helping us understand what's happening. If you feel angry, it often means that someone has treated you in a way you don't like.

If you feel calm, it usually means that you're somewhere you know well, with people you feel comfy around.

Sometimes our emotions get so big that we do things to try to make them smaller. We might cry to help with sadness, run fast to help with excitement, or clench our fists to help with anger.

All emotions are okay to feel.

> **All emotions are okay, but not all actions are. It's not okay to hurt your body, other people, or animals, or property—under any circumstances. If you feel this way, you can talk about your feelings with a trusted adult.**

ACTIVITY: FEELINGS WHEEL

There are so many emotions! How are you feeling right now? Can you find it on the feelings wheel?

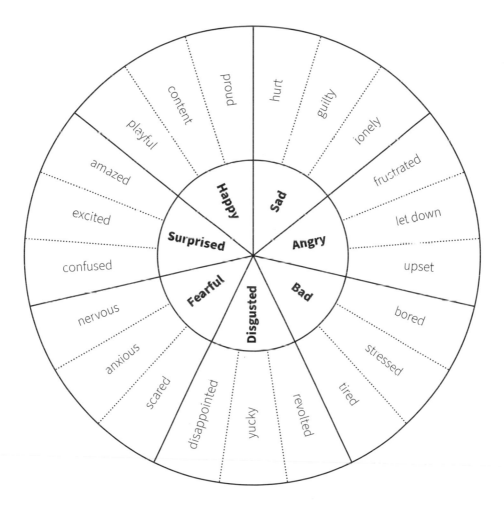

WHAT IS A POSITIVE OR NEGATIVE WORLDVIEW?

A "worldview" is the way you think about the world and your place in it. Everyone has one, and it's a bit like a pair of invisible glasses that you wear all the time.

Positive worldview	Negative worldview
People are mostly kind	People are mostly mean
Everyone is different and that's okay	Everyone should be the same or there's something wrong
It's okay to make mistakes	If I make a mistake, I have failed
I am lucky	I am unlucky
I feel okay with what I have	I am jealous of others

No one has a completely negative or completely positive worldview. We all see the world in a unique way, and it can change depending on our emotions. If you're feeling happy and positive, the world will look like a friendly, interesting place. If you're feeling negative and afraid, it will seem dark and frightening. We can start to see the world in a more positive light any time by being kind to ourselves, asking for help, and doing things that make us feel good.

ACTIVITY:
WHICH SITUATIONS MAKE ME FEEL NEGATIVE?

Different places or people can have a big effect on us and we can feel in a bad mood in certain situations. Perhaps it's a particular lesson at school or a place you go to with your family. Sometimes it's difficult to tell why some things make us feel like that. . . . They just do!

Can you think of a time when you felt pretty bad about yourself? Where were you? Who else was there? What happened?

Write about it here:

Thinking about the situations and places where we feel upset, negative, or grumpy can help us learn about our emotions. If you know you might start to feel negative, you can be prepared!

I AM KIND TO MYSELF AND OTHERS

WHAT IS SELF-TALK?

Imagine having someone with you all the time, commenting on the things you do and say, as well as how you look and feel. If that person was happy, encouraging, and positive—like a best friend—how would that feel?

What about if that person was negative and rude, and made you feel embarrassed about yourself?

Self-talk works just like that, but it's a voice that lives in your mind. It's the way you speak to and about yourself. If your self-talk is negative, it's a bit like having a bully with you all the time.

You can make your self-talk kinder and more positive, even when you're feeling big or tricky emotions.

Write down what you would say to a good friend who is feeling sad below. It might be: "I'm here for you," or "It's okay to cry."

Try saying those words to yourself next time *you* feel sad.

ACTIVITY:
COMPLIMENTS TO MYSELF

Can you think of some nice things to say to yourself? Fill in the speech bubbles with some positive compliments...

Next time you're feeling low and need a boost, come back to this page for some instant positivity!

PART 2:
POSITIVITY BOOSTERS

You've learned that everyone feels a mix of positive and negative feelings. Although negative feelings are okay and important, sometimes you want to feel more positive.

In this chapter, we'll learn some quick and fun ways to boost your positivity.

ACTIVITY:
POSITIVE OR NEGATIVE?

When do you feel most positive? And when do you feel most negative?

Color in the shapes below. Use red for things that make you feel negative (that could be sad, angry, or worried), yellow for the things that are about in the middle, and green for the things that feel positive and fun to you.

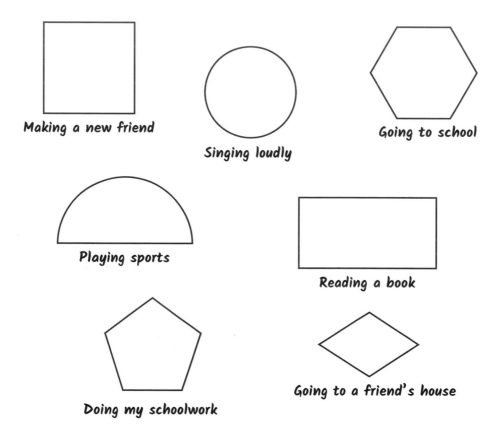

Making a new friend

Singing loudly

Going to school

Playing sports

Reading a book

Doing my schoolwork

Going to a friend's house

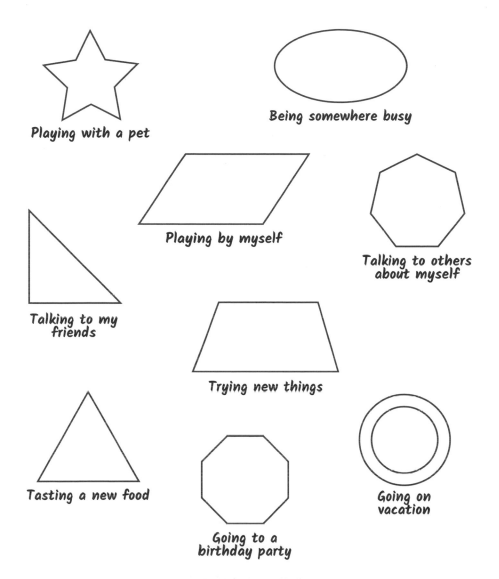

Playing with a pet

Being somewhere busy

Playing by myself

Talking to others about myself

Talking to my friends

Trying new things

Tasting a new food

Going to a birthday party

Going on vacation

Everyone is different, and something that feels really tricky for you might feel good to someone else. If your friend did this activity, this page might look quite different—and that's okay.

LISTEN TO YOUR BODY

Your body can tell you all sorts of things, without using words! If you feel positive when you're with someone, it can be a sign that they're a good fit to be your friend. If somewhere you go fills you with negative feelings, it's often a sign that something's not quite right.

The way your body gives you this information using emotions is called intuition. Sometimes intuition can feel small and quiet like a mouse, while other times it might be huge and loud like a lion. There are always lots of sensations going on in your body: emotions, your heart beating, food being digested, as well as things you can touch, smell, taste, and hear.

> **Close your eyes for a moment and notice what you can feel happening in your body right now. There's no need to write anything down or give it names—just notice.**

ACTIVITY: HOW DO YOU FEEL RIGHT NOW?

How positive or negative do you feel right at this moment? You might like to think about how this book is making you feel or perhaps about something you'll be doing later on today. Circle a number on the scale, and jot down a few words to help you remember what was going on when you chose it.

0   1   2   3   4   5   6   7   8   9   10

Really negative   *Really positive*

Come back to this activity another time, when you're feeling really positive:

0   1   2   3   4   5   6   7   8   9   10

Really negative   *Really positive*

. . . and one more time when you're feeling pretty negative:

0   1   2   3   4   5   6   7   8   9   10

Really negative   *Really positive*

Noticing how you feel at different times will help you see how your mood can go up and down, depending on what's happening.

WHAT IS MINDFULNESS?

Mindfulness means paying close attention to what is happening right at this moment. There are lots of ways to be mindful. Here are just a few:

- **Walk mindfully:** go really slow and feel how the ground feels beneath your feet. What textures can you feel?

- **Eat mindfully:** concentrate on the taste, smell, and feel of the food in your mouth; enjoy every mouthful.

- **Breathe mindfully:** feel the air go in through your nostrils, fill your lungs, and come out through your mouth. Keep concentrating on these feelings for three breaths.

- **Explore mindfully:** look around you as you walk somewhere (it could be a place that's new to you or one you know well) and notice all the little details.

- **Be mindfully creative:** give all your attention to what you are making or drawing, using all your senses to enjoy it.

If you're feeling negative about something that happened in the past, or something that could happen in the future, mindfulness is a brilliant way to help you let go of those difficult feelings.

ACTIVITY: MINDFUL COLORING

Color in the picture, taking notice of the colors you use and the feel of the pencil or pen in your hand. It's okay to color outside the lines or add details of your own.

ACTIVITY: CREATE A CUDDLE BOX

For a positivity boost, try making a box filled with things that feel comforting and positive.

You will need:

- A shoebox or a similar-size box

- Craft materials for decoration, e.g., paints, wrapping paper or stickers, glue, scissors

Instructions:

1. Ask your grown-up to help you remove the lid from your box.
2. Using paint or colorful pens, write your name in big letters on the lid, and decorate it and the rest of the box with your craft materials.
3. Fill your cuddle box with positive things. See below for lots of ideas!

What will you put in your cuddle box? Write your ideas on the next page.

Ideas for your cuddle box: a cool stone; photographs of people you love; a soft teddy; a note from a friend; a fidget toy; a piece of interesting fabric; a drawing of a pet; this book!

ACTIVITY: POSITIVE STEPS

We don't usually whizz from positive to negative and back again—that would be exhausting! If you want to change your mood, it's best to do it one step at a time, getting a little bit more positive with each step.

Chip's friend has moved to a different town, and Chip is feeling down in the dumps! It's sad when people move away, so it's no wonder Chip is feeling like this. Chip's sad feeling is bringing negative thoughts. Can you help Chip become just one step more positive? Choose one of these thoughts for Chip:

Bop was such a good friend—of course I feel sad that Bop's gone. I'll be okay and I know I have other good friends to play with, too.

It was wrong of Bop to move away. Bop's a bad friend.

I'm totally happy. I don't even need friends!

One of these thoughts is more negative, one of them is a step more positive, and one is way too positive!

Pretending to be completely positive when it doesn't match how you feel inside doesn't help. Being honest about your feelings means that the people around you will be able to get to know you better. It also helps you let the negative feelings go.

MY FEELINGS MATTER

ACTIVITY: I CAN TALK ABOUT MY FEELINGS

Talking about your emotions is like magic! Just saying them out loud can make you feel so much better. But it can feel scary to talk about feelings, maybe because you're worried that they don't matter or you wonder what the other person might think.

Is there something that's bothering you, but you find it hard to talk about? It might be something that's happened to you or another person, or something you're worried about. You can write or draw about it here.

If you feel comfortable, you could show this page to a trusted adult.

IT'S OKAY TO FEEL NEGATIVE EMOTIONS AND THINK NEGATIVE THOUGHTS

Everybody in the entire world has negative thoughts and feelings. Even cats and dogs, doctors, astronauts, and farmers. They are a part of being alive, just like positive thoughts and feelings.

If you try to squish them down, negative thoughts and feelings will just get more stuck inside you. So it's best to let them out!

The way we do that is important. Letting them out in a way that's unkind or hurts other people is like trying to give negative feelings to others.

If we let our emotions out by talking about how we feel or moving our bodies, the emotions can gently float away when they're ready, like fluffy clouds.

ACTIVITY: MOOD TRACKER

Keeping track of your feelings is a great way to get to know yourself better.
Pick a color for each mood:

Sad

Positive

Bored

Negative

Happy

_____

Angry

Use the colors you've picked to color in this mood tracker. Keep it going for two
weeks and see what you notice.

MOOD TRACKER

	Mon	Tue	Wed	Thu	Fri	Sat	Sun
Morning							
Afternoon							
Evening							
Night							

MOOD TRACKER

	Mon	Tue	Wed	Thu	Fri	Sat	Sun
Morning							
Afternoon							
Evening							
Night							

Are there some days that are harder than others? Perhaps there are times of the day when you feel at your best?

If you want to keep tracking your mood, you could trace the tracker onto a piece of paper or copy it into a notebook.

POSITIVE AFFIRMATIONS

Affirmations are positive statements that remind you of how brilliant you are. They can make you feel more positive in a flash!

Try saying these to yourself:

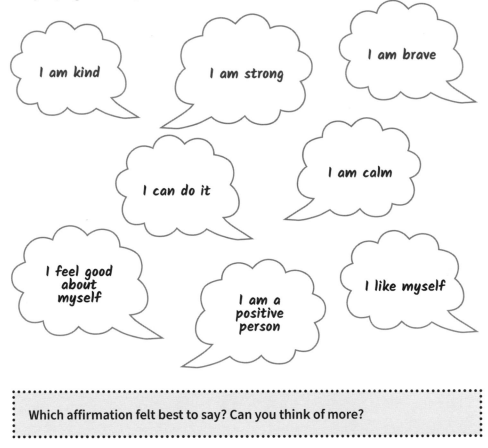

Which affirmation felt best to say? Can you think of more?

I'VE

GOT

THIS

ACTIVITY: BREATHING EXERCISES

Taking a deep breath is a quick way to give your positivity a boost. It brings more oxygen into your body, making you feel calm and strong.

Did you know that you can use shapes for breathing? Imagining a shape while you breathe makes your breaths longer and deeper.

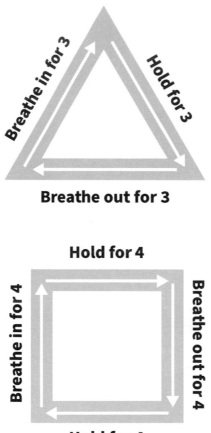

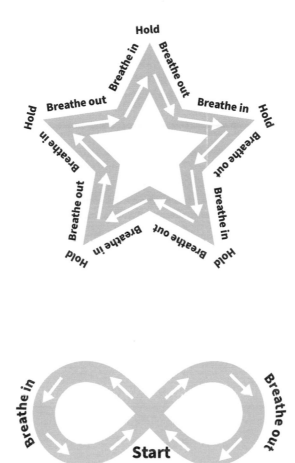

Hold

Breathe in   Breathe out

Breathe out   Breathe in

Hold   Hold

Breathe in   Breathe out

Breathe out   Breathe in

Hold   Hold

Breathe out   Breathe in

Breathe in

Breathe out

Start

ACTIVITY: MAKE A POSTER

Choose one of the shapes from the previous pages and make it into a poster to remind people how to take a deep breath.

You will need:

- Large piece of blank paper

- Pens, pencils, or paints

- Sticky tack

Instructions:

1. Take your paper and draw the shape nice and big in the middle. Don't forget to add instructions! Color your poster in or use paints so it stands out.
2. Stick it up in your house, using sticky tack, or at school if your teacher says it's okay!

ACTIVITY: I LIKE MYSELF

What are the best things about being you? Let's celebrate them here:

The kindest thing I've
ever done is . . .

The best thing
I've created is . . .

The bravest thing I've
ever done is . . .

I worked really
hard when . . .

I feel really
proud of . . .

ACTIVITY: FORTUNE TELLER

Make this positivity fortune teller and use it to play with your friends and family! Follow these instructions to fold your paper into a fun game. Ask a grown-up to help.

You will need:

- A square piece of paper

- Pens and pencils for coloring

Instructions:

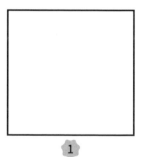

1

Start with a square piece of paper.

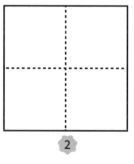

2

Fold and unfold along the dotted lines to find the middle.

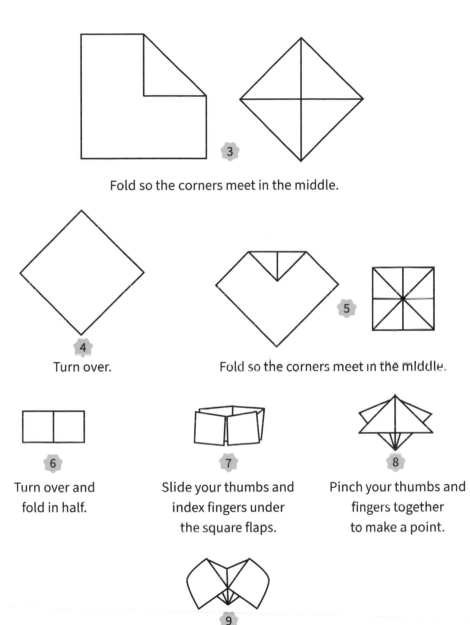

Fold so the corners meet in the middle.

Turn over.

Fold so the corners meet in the middle.

Turn over and fold in half.

Slide your thumbs and index fingers under the square flaps.

Pinch your thumbs and fingers together to make a point.

Your fortune teller is ready to decorate.

You can color in the outer squares or draw something different on each.

Inside, write numbers. Under the flaps, write a positive message. Here are some ideas:

Have a brilliant day
You are awesome
Be yourself
You're amazing
Go for it
You're a good friend
Superstar
You are brave

ACTIVITY: BUBBLE BREATHING

When Chip's feeling tricky emotions, he knows it's time to take some deep breaths. Chip likes to imagine blowing the world's biggest bubble. You can try it, too!

Take a deep breath to the count of three, in through your nose, and fill your lungs with oxygen.

Now purse your lips like you're going to blow a bubble. As you breathe out, imagine it growing bigger and bigger. Picture the rainbow swirls on its surface. When you've finished breathing out, imagine it floating gently up to the sky as you breathe in again, ready to blow another gigantic bubble.

REMEMBER TO PRESS PAUSE

If you're feeling negative, down, or upset, a simple way of boosting positivity is to imagine pressing pause on your mind.

When you press pause, all negative or upsetting thoughts can stop. You can take big, deep breaths. You can ask for help.

ACTIVITY: POSITIVITY TOOLKIT

In this chapter, we've looked at loads of different ways to boost positivity. It's okay if some work for you and others don't—that's because we're all different!

Imagine building a toolkit of all the things that help you feel more positive. What would go in yours?

Write your best positivity tools here:

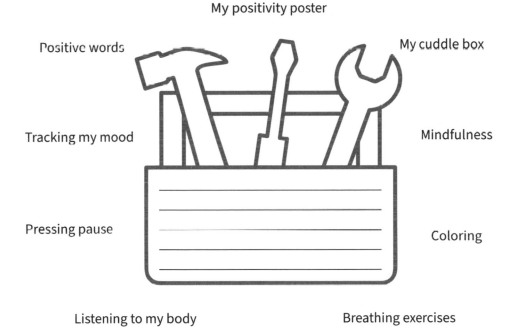

My positivity poster

Positive words

My cuddle box

Tracking my mood

Mindfulness

Pressing pause

Coloring

Listening to my body

Breathing exercises

Talking about my feelings

PART 3: NEGATIVITY SHRINKERS

Sometimes negative thoughts and feelings can get really big in your mind. In this chapter, we'll learn some brilliant ways to shrink negativity down to size.

YOU ARE NOT ALONE

When you're struggling with negativity, it can feel like you're the only one. The truth is, everyone feels down or negative sometimes. We mostly only show these feelings to our families and maybe close friends—and some people don't show anyone at all.

Because of this, it can seem like everyone else is fine all the time and you're the only one with difficult feelings. But if you think about it, unless you show or talk about your emotions with others, they won't know how you're feeling. . . . And if other people don't show or tell you their emotions, you don't really know how they are feeling, either.

It might feel frustrating, calming, or surprising to learn this!

ACTIVITY: WHAT ARE MY SKILLS?

Think about the things you are really good at. What popped into your head first?

_____

_____

_____

Sports and school subjects are not the only things you can be good at—but if you have these kinds of skills, that's wonderful! Also, think about friendship skills, the kinds of art you like to make, what you're good at imagining, what you do for fun, and how you help others. . . .

Can you write some more of your skills?

_____

_____

_____

Keep adding to this list as you remember or discover new skills. Thinking hard about the things you feel positive about is a great way to shrink negativity.

ACTIVITY: ROOM FOR ALL MY EMOTIONS

There is room in your heart for every type of emotion. When you remember this, it's a little bit easier to deal with difficult feelings and feel positive about being you.

Can you color and decorate each section of the heart on the next page to show the different emotions? Think about which colors might match each one.

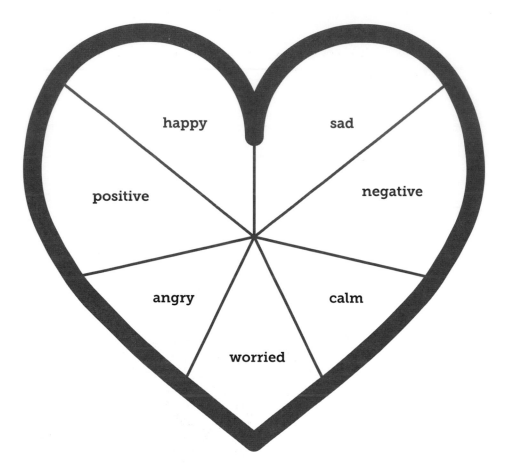

TALKING ABOUT YOUR THOUGHTS AND FEELINGS

Talking to someone about your feelings might feel super uncomfortable! There are lots of ways to make it easier, though. Here are just a few ideas:

Write about them in a letter

Talk while walking together

Make up silly voices to use when you speak

Use emojis

Talk while you're tidying up together

Talk at bedtime

Hide under a blanket together

Role-play with your favorite toys

ACTIVITY: WHO CAN I TALK TO?

Who feels good to talk to? Not just about big feelings and difficult stuff, but also about fun and normal things.

Write down who you know you can talk to:

_____

_____

_____

_____

_____

_____

_____

_____

_____

_____

_____

_____

_____

_____

_____

_____

_____

_____

_____

_____

ACTIVITY: BODY MAP

This exercise will help you relax, quiet negative thoughts, and even fall asleep more easily. You can try it when you're lying comfortably in bed—read it to yourself out loud, or ask someone to read it to you in their most calming voice:

Close your eyes and imagine your body is an island. Your hair is a beautiful sea. Your boat comes to rest on forehead beach and you step out, ready to explore. You feel the smoothness of your nose and explore the curly shells that are your ears on either side. You sit on your chin for a rest, before jumping down and listening to the ground to hear your heart beating. You call down into your belly button and hear an echo! You scale the tall leg mountains until you reach your knees at the top, then you slide down the other side. You sit on your toes, which are covered in soft moss. You dangle your legs over the side and take three deep breaths.

Taking time to relax and pay attention to your body like this helps your brain calm down and grow positivity.

I CAN DO
MY BEST

ACTIVITY: EXPRESSING ANGER

Just like smiling when you're happy or jumping up and down when you're excited, emotions such as anger can be shown on the outside!

The tricky thing about anger is that, when the feeling gets really big, it can make you want to behave in ways that frighten, hurt, or upset others. So, how can you let out emotions in a way that feels okay for everyone?

The key is to listen to your body. For example, when you feel angry, your body might want to kick. Kicking people or animals is never okay, because it hurts them—and things shouldn't be kicked either, because they might break and you could hurt yourself. So if your body wants to kick, you need to find a way to let out those feelings without hurting anyone or breaking anything.

Write about or draw the angry feelings in your body. When I feel angry, my body wants to . . .

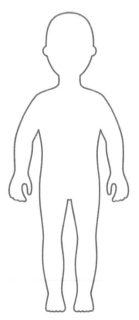

Angry body feelings	What you can do to let them out
Kicking, running	Jump up and down, stomp your feet, drum your hands on your legs, bounce on a trampoline, kick a soccer ball into a goal
Hitting, throwing	Drum your hands on a cushion or sofa, sweep your arms up and down, squeeze a cushion
Shouting, unkind words	Say: "I feel angry!", hum into your belly, write down unkind words, say silly words, sing an angry song
Crying, hiding, and curling up small	Ask for a hug or hug yourself, cry (it's always okay to cry!), take some deep breaths, squeeze something soft

ACTIVITY: GET TO KNOW YOUR INNER MEANIE

On page 31, we learned about self-talk. The way you talk to and about yourself plays a big part in how positive or negative you feel.

If you sometimes have quite negative self-talk, you have an inner meanie! Don't worry: most people do.

Think about a time when you made a mistake. Did your inner meanie say anything to you? If it did, can you remember some of the words it used? It might be something like: "I'm stupid," or "I always get it wrong."

_____

_____

_____

_____

_____

If someone said that to your best friend, what would you think?

_____

_____

_____

_____

_____

No one deserves to be spoken to unkindly, even if the voice comes from inside them. It can be tricky to speak to yourself with more kindness and positivity but getting to know the voice inside you is the first step.

Imagine if you could see that inner meanie—what color would it be? Would it be furry or smooth, or with spikes all over?

Try drawing your inner meanie here:

Have fun with this exercise. There's no right or wrong answer! You're the expert on what it's like to be you.

I HAVE
COURAGE

ACTIVITY: GRATITUDE JOURNAL

Gratitude means feeling thankful. A gratitude journal is like a diary of all the positive things that happened to you. Taking a little bit of time each day to think of three things you're grateful for trains your brain to find positivity.

Before bed is a good time to write down those three things. Jot them down here. There's a bonus idea every day, if you get stuck!

Monday

1._____
2._____
3._____

Did you smell any delicious scents today?

Tuesday

1._____
2._____
3._____

What was the yummiest thing you ate today?

Wednesday
1._____
2._____
3._____

Who did you enjoy talking to today?

Thursday
1._____
2._____
3._____

What was interesting today?

Friday
1._____
2._____
3._____

What did you read today?

Saturday

1. _____

2. _____

3. _____

What made you laugh today?

Sunday

1. _____

2. _____

3. _____

What made you feel special today?

If you enjoyed keeping a gratitude journal, you could use a notebook or normal diary to keep it going!

DON'T COMPARE YOURSELF TO OTHERS

Everyone is different, special, and unique. There isn't one perfect way to be, even if it feels like that sometimes.

Like ingredients in a cake, all different kinds of people together make life colorful and interesting. You can't make a cake from just one kind of ingredient!

That's why comparing yourself to other children isn't worth it—you are special because you are you, and others are special for being themselves. If someone tries to make you feel negative about yourself because you are different from them in some way, that's unfair and wrong of them. You are just right, exactly as you are.

I AM
STRONG

ACTIVITY: MY HAPPY PLACE

Think of a place where you feel happy, relaxed, and positive. It might be somewhere you go every day, somewhere you've only visited once or a place from your imagination—or a mix of all three!

What is the name of your happy place?

_____

_____

_____

What sounds can you hear there?

_____

_____

_____

Are there other people or animals?

_____

_____

_____

What scents can you smell?

_____

_____

_____

What is there to eat and drink?

_____

_____

_____

Let's draw your happy place here:

Picturing your happy place helps your mind and body relax and feel more positive.

Take a minute to do a quick meditation. It will help you feel relaxed. You can read it to yourself in your head or ask someone to read it to you.

Make sure you're sitting comfortably. Take a deep breath in through your nose, and let it out through your nose. As you breathe in again, imagine pulling the breath all the way down into your belly, blowing it up like a balloon. Then slowly let the air out of the balloon and out through your nose. Keep breathing like this.

Picture yourself in your happy place. It's summer there, and the air is lovely and warm. Take a moment to picture as many details as you can: the colors, the plants, what the ground is like. As you breathe out, you push a gentle breeze across your happy place. As you breathe in, you smell all the wonderful smells.

On your next breath out, the gentle breeze catches a beautiful green leaf. You blow it high up into the sky. As you breathe in, it floats slowly back down toward you.

You sit on the soft ground and let the leaf drift down into your hands. Take another deep breath in, and out.

> **Scientists have found that meditating like this helps you to feel more positive!**

ACTIVITY: JOURNEY STICK

Walking in nature is a brilliant way to build positivity. Did you know that trees actually release special chemicals that make you feel calmer and more positive as you walk by them?

Next time you go on a walk, try making a journey stick for some extra fun.

You will need:

- A ball of string

- A good, strong stick about the length of your forearm

Instructions:

1. Tie your string firmly to your stick, near one end.
2. As you walk, look for nature finds on the ground like fallen leaves, twigs, feathers, pieces of lichen.
3. Fix them to your stick by winding the string tightly around each one. By the end of your walk, you'll have a beautiful journey stick, covered in treasures.

ACTIVITY: GET CREATIVE

There's no right or wrong way to be creative. The best creations happen when you let your pens and pencils wander freely across the page, just having fun with the shapes and colors you make.

Use this page to let your creativity run wild:

Have fun and don't worry about trying to make it perfect. If you make a mistake, can you turn it into part of the picture? Your drawing is beautiful because you made it!

I HAVE
BRILLIANT
IDEAS

YOU'RE DOING GREAT!

Learning about positivity and negativity can be difficult and confusing! It might feel like you need to change something about yourself in order to be "positive enough," but that's simply not true. You are just right, exactly as you are.

Finding out how your mind works gives you the power to understand yourself and feel positive about being you.

I'm doing great

ACTIVITY: POSITIVELY IMPERFECT

There's no such thing as perfect, because everyone is different. Our differences are what makes the world interesting and fun.

Here's a game that creates great pictures out of imperfections—what looks random or even like a mistake turns into something inspiring! Play it by yourself or ask a friend to join in.

Take a pen or pencil and close your eyes. Scribble in the square below for about two seconds.

Now, open your eyes and pick a pen or pencil in a different color (if you're playing with a friend, swap pictures).

Take a look at your scribble. Can you see any shapes in it? Perhaps an animal, a building, or a tree. . . .

With your colored pen or pencil, add details (like eyes, paws, or chimneys) to your scribble to make it into a picture.

MY TOP NEGATIVITY SHRINKERS

Wow! We've learned so many ways to shrink negativity. What were the best ones for you? Perhaps your happy place makes you feel calm, or being creative is the best way for you to let your worries out. Write down your top negativity shrinkers here:

When I feel down, I can . . .

_____

_____

_____

_____

_____

_____

When I feel angry, I can . . .

_____

_____

_____

_____

_____

_____

When I feel worried, I can . . .

_____

_____

_____

_____

_____

_____

PART 4: LOOKING AFTER YOURSELF

The better your body feels, the easier it is to feel positive. Think about it: when you're tired, hungry, or thirsty, that's when it's easiest to feel negative.

In this chapter, we're going to learn all about taking care of your body and mind.

WHY IT'S IMPORTANT TO RELAX

Have you heard of the nervous system? It sounds like a kind of worried computer, but it's actually a part of your body. The nervous system is a complicated web of cells and neurons that connects every part of your body to your brain.

When you're feeling big feelings, that means your nervous system is activated and working hard. It's important to give it regular breaks, so it doesn't get too tired. When you relax, that's exactly what happens: your nervous system relaxes, too.

ACTIVITY: CHILL-OUT ZONE

Imagine a secret den that only you know about and can visit when you want to chill out. What would it be made of? Where would it be? How would you decorate it?

Use your imagination to design your perfect chill-out den:

ACTIVITY: WATER TRACKER

Have you ever seen a plant that needs a drink? Its leaves droop, its petals curl, and its stem turns pale and weak. Human beings aren't so different: we need water to feel our best, just like plants.

Set yourself a challenge to drink six glasses of water a day—that's how much is best for a child your age.

Keep track of your water-drinking here:

WATER TRACKER

Monday	⬇⬇⬇⬇⬇⬇
Tuesday	⬇⬇⬇⬇⬇⬇
Wednesday	⬇⬇⬇⬇⬇⬇
Thursday	⬇⬇⬇⬇⬇⬇
Friday	⬇⬇⬇⬇⬇⬇
Saturday	⬇⬇⬇⬇⬇⬇
Sunday	⬇⬇⬇⬇⬇⬇

MY BODY IS PRECIOUS

LOVING AND RESPECTING YOUR BODY

Chip's body is furry and orange, and Chip feels positive about it!

Your body belongs to you and deserves to be looked after properly. You can show your body love by keeping yourself clean, drinking enough water (turn to page 93 to track how much water you drink), eating when you feel hungry, and asking for help if you're hurt.

It doesn't matter what your body looks like to others. Feeling positive about your body means treating it with kindness and respect.

ACTIVITY: YES AND NO

"No" is a really important word, just like "yes!" When we say yes and no, we let others around us know how we feel and what we want.

But sometimes it can feel scary to tell others what we really think—perhaps you worry about hurting someone's feelings or not being positive enough. The truth is, saying what you feel is always a positive choice.

Chip feels nervous. Chip doesn't feel like hugging, but Chip's friend wants to hug. Chip doesn't want to hurt anyone's feelings. Can you think of different ways for Chip to say "no"?

Chip's friend didn't realize that Chip didn't want a hug. It's great that Chip found the bravery to say so. A hug is no good if one of the huggers doesn't like it!

HEALTHY EATING

Eating a balanced diet that's full of healthy things will help your body keep well and strong. The healthier and more well-nourished your body is, the more positive you'll feel.

What kinds of food does your body need every day to be strong and healthy?

- Carbohydrates for energy, like potatoes, bread, and pasta

- Protein to heal and grow, like eggs, fish, and beans

- Fats to store energy, like butter, nuts, and cheese

- Fiber to help your digestive system to work, like fruit and vegetables

- It's also okay to have a few treats, like ice cream or chocolate

ACTIVITY: EASY BANANA PANCAKES

These banana pancakes are packed with protein, fiber, and healthy carbohydrates, so they're great for breakfast or a snack! Ask a grown-up to help you with the recipe. Makes four small pancakes.

You will need:

- 1 ripe banana

- 1 egg

- 1 heaped tablespoon whole wheat flour

- Oil for cooking

Instructions:

1 Mash the banana in a bowl, and then stir in the egg and flour.
2 Ask an adult to help you heat a little oil in a frying pan. When small bubbles start to form, spoon some of the pancake mixture into the pan to form four pancakes.
3 When you see bubbles on the surface of the pancakes, it's time to carefully flip them over. Once they're golden brown on both sides, they're ready to serve.

ACTIVITY: MOVE YOUR BODY

Scientists have found that exercise not only makes your body feel good, but also makes your brain healthier! Moving your body will make you feel calmer, happier, and more positive.

That's because the movement from exercise calms the part of the brain that's in charge of emotions: the amygdala. At the same time, the brain releases chemicals that make you feel great all over.

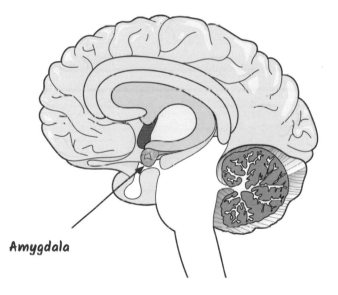

Amygdala

Moving your body makes you feel great! Try these exercises first thing in the morning to kick-start your day.

Stretch up to the ceiling like a tree

Swing your arms like a windmill

Wriggle your body like a fish

Tap your legs like a drum

POSITIVITY AT HOME

Where we are has a big effect on how we feel. We spend a lot of our time at home, so making it a positive place is a good idea.

Here are some simple tips for growing positivity at home.

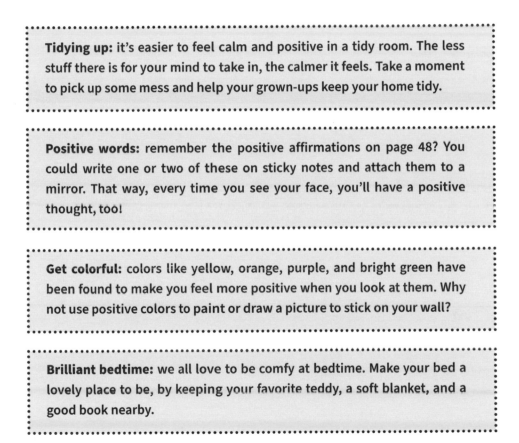

Tidying up: it's easier to feel calm and positive in a tidy room. The less stuff there is for your mind to take in, the calmer it feels. Take a moment to pick up some mess and help your grown-ups keep your home tidy.

Positive words: remember the positive affirmations on page 48? You could write one or two of these on sticky notes and attach them to a mirror. That way, every time you see your face, you'll have a positive thought, too!

Get colorful: colors like yellow, orange, purple, and bright green have been found to make you feel more positive when you look at them. Why not use positive colors to paint or draw a picture to stick on your wall?

Brilliant bedtime: we all love to be comfy at bedtime. Make your bed a lovely place to be, by keeping your favorite teddy, a soft blanket, and a good book nearby.

POSITIVITY SCAVENGER HUNT

Can you find something in your home for each item on the list?

- Something you're grateful for

- Something you were given as a gift

- Something you made yourself

- Something you really treasure

- Something that smells good

- Something that keeps you warm

- Something that reminds you of a happy memory

- Something that makes you feel calm

If you look for positivity, you'll find it!

I CAN TAKE A DEEP BREATH

POSITIVITY ONLINE

The internet is an incredible invention: it gives you access to so much fun and learning. It's important to use this tool in a positive way, and that means staying safe online.

Remember the rules for keeping safe and positive on the internet:

- Never post your personal information or passwords online

- Never befriend someone you don't know

- Never meet up with someone you've met online

- Think carefully before you post pictures or words online

- If you see something that makes you feel uncomfortable, scared, or worried, you should always ask a trusted adult for help

- Remember to be just as kind online as you would be in real life

ACTIVITY: WEEKLY PLANNER

Making sure you spend time away from screens is really important. Studies have found that children who limit their screen time and spend plenty of time outdoors feel much more positive about themselves, learn better, and worry less. Ask your grown-up to help you plan in screen time, outdoor time, and time together each week.

	Monday	Tuesday	Wednesday	Thursday	Friday	Saturday	Sunday
Morning							
Lunchtime							
Afternoon							
Evening							

PART 5: FINDING POSITIVITY EVERY DAY

You've learned so much about positivity! In this chapter, we're going to find out all the ways you can feel positive about yourself every day.

ALL ABOUT POSITIVITY

Take a moment to recap what we've learned about positivity so far.

Positivity is . . .	Positivity is not . . .
Feeling okay with all emotions	Feeling happy all the time
Looking for small, good things	Ignoring things that are sad or difficult
Treating others with respect	Always saying yes
Treating yourself with respect	Ignoring your problems
Learning from mistakes	Always getting it right

ACTIVITY: MY POSITIVE DAY

What would a really positive, feel-good day be like for you? Think about all the things that you'd do and the people you'd see.

Write about or draw your super-positive day here:

STORIES OF POSITIVITY

Sophie, 9

"All my friends have great singing voices, but I don't like how mine sounds. I always felt awkward when they'd sing together, thinking I would ruin it if I joined in. One day they were singing my absolute favorite song and I decided to just go for it, so I sang, too. It was fun and no one thought my singing was bad or got annoyed with me. I feel much more comfortable singing now."

Ben, 8

"A group of kids I hang around with always made fun of my curly hair. When I got upset, they said it was just a joke and laughed at me more for getting upset. I spoke to my mom about it and she said my feelings matter, even if it's only supposed to be a joke. So I told them it's not funny and that they should stop doing it."

Grace, 11

"When I saw a kid smaller than me being bullied, I thought I shouldn't do anything because I'm not big or tough. But when I saw how upset the kid was, I realized I could make a difference. I told the bullies to leave him alone and I made sure he was okay."

Rafif, 11

" I've always felt a bit embarrassed about not liking scary movies. I managed to keep it a secret until a sleepover last year. My friend wanted to watch one and I felt really nervous, but I found the courage to say I didn't want to. It was fine, and we watched something funny that we both enjoyed instead. "

Harry, 9

" I used to hate going to school. Every day I'd wake up with a heavy feeling in my chest. It wasn't anything in particular that I hated—everything just felt boring and difficult. I talked to my caregiver about it, and with her help, as well as the help of my brother and teachers, I slowly began to feel better. Nothing much about school has changed, but the way I think and feel about it is really different now. "

Ethan, 10

" I used to have a group of friends who were always looking for something wrong with the way I look and pointing it out. They made me feel ugly and boring, but I only felt that way when I was with those friends. So I tried spending less time with them and it felt great. I've got better friends now. "

TAKE IT SLOW

One of the most powerful ways to build a positive worldview is to understand that everything takes time. So, you're not an expert at speaking Spanish, or rock climbing, or baking . . . but with practice, anything will start to feel easier.

When you think about things in this way, the world feels a lot more positive. Even when something goes wrong, you can see it as a useful lesson you would never have learned if things had gone according to plan.

Skills, friendships, new habits—even positivity!—are all things built slowly, one brick at a time. If you find a way to add a little bit every day, soon you'll have built something wonderful.

I CAN MAKE A DIFFERENCE

ACTIVITY: RANDOM ACTS OF KINDNESS

You can be kind and positive every day in little ways. Here are just a few ideas:

- Paint a stone with a positive message and leave it somewhere public for someone else to find—it might just make their day!

- Save a bee: if you see a tired bee on the ground, mix two teaspoons of sugar with one teaspoon of water to make a syrup. Put a blob near the bee so it will drink it and get some energy to fly back to its hive.

- When you enjoy a meal, tell the person who cooked it how delicious it was.

- Plant a tree.

- Give your sandwich crumbs to the birds.

- Make a thank-you card for your bus driver, trash collectors, or teacher.

- Leave a positive note in a library book.

- Make a funny video for your family.

- Draw pet portraits for your neighbors.

Hold the door open for someone.

Bring frozen peas and oats to feed the ducks (these are the healthiest duck foods!).

Pass on a book you enjoyed to a friend.

Can you add any more?

_____

_____

_____

_____

_____

_____

_____

_____

OK

OK

ACTIVITY: BECOME AN EXPERT LISTENER

Listening is one of the most powerful things you can do to help others feel positive about themselves. When you listen well, the person talking feels respected and knows that their feelings matter to you.

Can you think of a time when you listened well? Write about it here:

_____

_____

_____

_____

_____

_____

_____

_____

_____

Can you think of a time when someone really listened to you? Write about it here:

_____

_____

_____

_____

_____

_____

_____

_____

_____

_____

Color in Chip's body parts that are needed for listening:

Eyes: looking at
the person talking

Ears: hearing
what they
are saying

Brain: thinking about
what they
are saying

Heart: caring
about what they
are saying

Hands: calm

Mouth: quiet

Body: facing the
person talking

Feet: still

I AM A GOOD FRIEND

POSITIVELY DIFFERENT

We are all completely unique. Some people find it easier to "fit in" and match those around them, while others feel like they stand out wherever they go.

The way you look, how you act, the things you're interested in, and the way you think are a special combination that make you, you. Perhaps one, or more, of these things about you is quite unusual—that can feel tricky, but you should never be made to feel bad because you are different.

Our differences make life interesting and fun.

Some people find it difficult to respect those who are not the same as them. They worry that differences are a negative thing and a problem. If you happen to meet someone like this, their worries are not your problem to solve. You are awesome just as you are.

We should all respect each other and ourselves. So, if someone's not showing you respect, you can walk away from them.

LET YOUR VOICE BE HEARD

Your ideas are unique to you. It might sometimes feel scary to talk about them with others, but sharing ideas is how amazing things happen.

Every invention, book, TV show, and piece of art exists because someone had a brilliant idea and was brave enough to share it.

When you feel positive about yourself, you'll be able to find the courage to share your thoughts and ideas.

ACTIVITY: HOW YOU CAN MAKE A DIFFERENCE

Do you think you're too small to make a positive difference? It's not true! There are lots of ways you can spread positivity and make the world a better place.

- Collect plastic to make eco bricks

- Sell your old toys to raise money for charity

- Make compost

- Make a bug hotel

- Collect clothes for charity

- Make a wild patch in your garden

- Bake cakes for your teacher

- Collect food for a food bank

Is there something on that list that you'd like to try? Make a plan here—who could help you? What will you need?

_____

_____

_____

_____

_____

_____

_____

_____

_____

_____

_____

_____

_____

_____

_____

_____

_____

_____

_____

_____

_____

_____

_____

_____

_____

_____

ACTIVITY: SING IT OUT LOUD

Singing is an excellent way to boost positivity for yourself and those around you. Hearing someone sing a happy song makes people feel a little bit happier, and it works the same with sad tunes!

Pick a song that makes you feel great, and write some of the lyrics here:

_____

_____

_____

_____

_____

_____

_____

_____

_____

_____

_____

Did you know that singing is really good for calming your body? When you sing, your vocal cords vibrate. They're really close to your brain stem, which is connected to your amygdala—we learned about it on page 99—and their vibrations will calm this part of the brain and your emotions.

ACTIVITY: MY FRIENDS

Who are your closest friends? You might have a lot, or you might have just one or two—and that's okay. We don't fit with everyone, so when it comes to friendships, having a small number of good ones is excellent.

Draw some of your friends here—what makes them a good friend? Can you think of three words to describe each one?

The people we spend time with make a big difference about how we feel about ourselves!

I CAN STAND UP FOR MYSELF

GOOD-FRIEND CHECKLIST

Do you know what makes a good friend? Take a look at this checklist so you can tell a good friend from a bad one.

A good friend . . .	A bad friend . . .
Says kind things to you	Says unkind things to you
Cares about your feelings	Doesn't care if they upset you
Never hurts you	Hurts you
Talks and listens to you	Ignores you
Includes you in their games	Leaves you out
Stands up for you	Makes fun of you
Is happy for you when something positive happens	Is jealous when you're happy
Says sorry if they do something wrong	Blames you for everything
Talks to you about it, if you've upset them	Stops talking to you without saying why

ACTIVITY: HOW ARE YOU DOING?

Take a moment to think about how you are feeling. What are you finding tricky at the moment? What makes you feel negative, worried, or scared? Write or draw about it here:

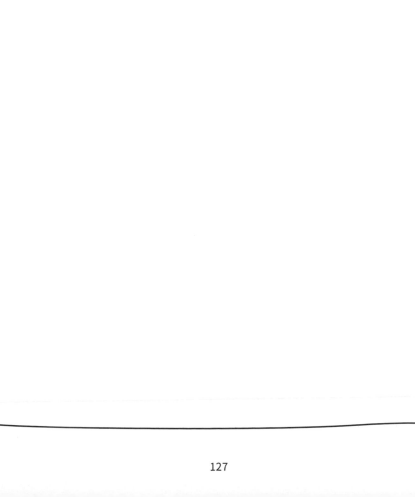

On this page, write or draw about the positive things in your life right now:

ACTIVITY: TURN A NEGATIVE INTO A POSITIVE

Chip was looking forward to a friend visiting this weekend, but the friend has just canceled. Chip feels upset: the weekend is ruined! After feeling sad and disappointed for a little while, Chip remembers all the things that are fun to do alone, like coloring in and reading adventure books. The weekend's not looking so bad now.

How do you solve problems? It can feel really difficult when something goes wrong. But if you follow these steps, you'll be able to turn a negative into a positive.

1. First, ask yourself three questions:
   What am I feeling?
   What is the problem?
   Do I need help to solve it?
2. Next, think about solutions—it's okay if you think of lots or just one!
3. Pick a solution

Can you think of a time you had a problem to solve?

_____

_____

_____

_____

How did you feel?

_____

_____

_____

_____

Did you ask for help? Who from?

_____

_____

_____

_____

How did you solve the problem?

_____

_____

_____

_____

If you had a time machine, would you go back and solve the problem in a different way?

_____

_____

_____

_____

PART 6: CELEBRATE YOURSELF

You've nearly reached the end of the book! In this chapter, we'll take a look back at all the things you've learned and think about how you can use them in your everyday life.

ACTIVITY: MAKE AN ACTION PLAN

Now you're bursting with loads of knowledge about positivity, it's time to put it into action. Think about all the activities and ideas in this book—or come up with some of your own!

When I'm feeling down and I'm ready to feel a bit better, I can . . .

_____

_____

_____

_____

To find positivity every day, I will . . .

_____

_____

_____

_____

To spread positivity, I can . . .

_____

_____

_____

_____

To be kind to myself, I will . . .

_____

_____

_____

_____

ACTIVITY: MAKE YOUR OWN POSITIVE STATEMENTS

Create an eye-catching positive statement to put on your wall, mirror, or fridge at home!

You will need:

- Colored card
- Pencil
- PVA glue
- Fine paintbrush
- Biodegradable glitter
- Old newspaper

Instructions:

1. Pick a positive statement that makes you feel calm, happy, and strong.
2. Write it in big, neat letters on a piece of colored card.
3. Use the paintbrush to carefully spread glue over the letters.
4. Sprinkle glitter over the glue and let it dry for about 30 seconds.
5. Tip the paper over some newspaper so all the leftover glitter slides off (you can then transfer the glitter back into its container).
6. Leave your positive statement to dry fully overnight.

> **Flip back through the book to find positive statements to use.**

POSITIVELY ME: GOLDEN RULES

All feelings are okay

You can make
mistakes

Be kind to yourself

Respect yourself
and others

Spread positivity

Talk about
your feelings

ACTIVITY: HELP CHIP THE MONSTER

Can you use the things you've learned in this book to help Chip out?

Chip is feeling down in the dumps. Everything seems to be difficult, boring, and negative, and it feels like nothing ever goes right for Chip!

Looking for small things to feel grateful for helps build positivity.

Can you spot five things that Chip could feel grateful for in the picture? Draw a circle around the ones you can find.

Did you spot any others?

Teddy, books, pet fish, comfy bed, building blocks, unicorn, ball, plant

The end

You've come to the very end of the book. Chip has learned a lot about positivity—have you?

Positivity is like a seesaw. Nothing is ever totally positive or totally negative—perhaps broccoli seems like a negative to you if you don't like the taste, but to your body, it's a healthy positive. The key is to find a balance: add to the positive side of your seesaw and other people's, while being kind to the negative side, too.

You can come back to this book any time you like—to boost your positivity or help a friend understand it a bit better. It's not easy, and you should be very proud of yourself. Well done for being positively you!

I AM
POSITIVELY
ME!

For parents and caregivers: How to help boost your child's positivity

Healthy positivity is more complicated than putting on a brave face and only showing positive emotions. It means accepting all feelings and expressing them in appropriate ways—that could mean telling a friend when they've upset us, looking for small positives when we're going through a hard time, or taking time to breathe deeply when we're getting angry. The same goes for children: the most positive child in the class is likely to be the one who feels comfortable expressing a full range of emotions.

The best way you can help your child to build a positive worldview is by encouraging them to express themselves and modeling healthy ways to do this. It might feel tempting to dismiss complaints or frustrations, asking your child to see the positive side of whatever is happening to them. But this can lead to them becoming more attached to their negative views; in the long run, they might simply stop talking about them with you.

When children feel able to express their negative thoughts and feelings, they have a chance to release pent-up frustration—just like a good vent after a tough week at work does. Listen openly and accept your child's emotions—even if you don't agree with their opinions, you can still validate how they feel. When you do this, your child feels understood and will be able to move past their initial frustration, see things more objectively, and even start to see positives.

By being a calm, empathetic listener, you will help your child grow emotionally secure and resilient. They'll become flexible thinkers, capable of seeing differing viewpoints and changing their minds.

I hope this book has been useful for you and your child. It can be so difficult to know how to respond to negativity, and you're doing a great job by being open to all of your child's feelings and helping them to feel positive about themselves.

Further advice

If you're worried about your child's mental health, do talk it through with your pediatrician. While almost all children experience feelings of shyness, some may need extra help. There are lots of great resources out there for information and guidance on children's mental health. Here are just a few:

CDC
www.cdc.gov
(800) 232-4636

APA
www.apa.org
(800) 374-2721

Childhelp
www.childhelp.org
(480) 922-8212

Child Mind Institute
www.childmind.org
(212) 308-3118

The Youth Mental Health Project
www.ymhproject.org
info@ymhproject.org

Recommended reading

For children:

Be Amazing! An Inspiring Guide to Being Your Own Champion by Chris Hoy
Walker Books, 2020

Happy, Healthy Minds: A Children's Guide to Emotional Wellbeing by The School of Life
The School of Life Press, 2020

The Feelings Book: The Care and Keeping of Your Emotions by Lynda Madison
American Girl Publishing, 2013

For adults:

The Gifts of Imperfection by Brené Brown
Hazelden Publishing, 2010

The Book You Wish Your Parents Had Read (and Your Children Will Be Glad That You Did) by Philippa Perry
Penguin, 2019

Image credits

pp.12, 13, 17, 19, 20, 21, 24, 28, 33, 36, 45, 52, 53, 57, 58, 60, 61, 62, 63, 65, 67, 77, 80, 82, 84, 86, 87, 90, 95, 96, 97, 100, 106, 111, 116, 118, 119, 129, 131, 135, 136 – monsters © mers1na/Shutterstock.com; p.13 – smiling sun © Maksym Drozd/Shutterstock.com; p.21 – flowers © Marnikus/Shutterstock.com; p.24 – trophy © mijatmijatovic/Shutterstock.com; p.24, 25 – bin © Lemonade Serenade/Shutterstock.com; p.26, 60, 63 – emoticons © SpicyTruffel/Shutterstock.com; p. 28 – umbrella © mijatmijatovic/Shutterstock.com; p.28 – rain cloud © mijatmijatovic/Shutterstock.com; pp.13, 32, 42, 48, 58, 60, 61, 62, 65, 86, 96 – bubbles © Paket/Shutterstock.com; p.33 – sun © Nikolaeva/Shutterstock.com; p.34, 35 – shapes © wilkastok/Shutterstock.com; p.39 – © Ekaterina kkch/Shutterstock.com; p.45 – storm cloud © MOSQUITO_vector/Shutterstock.com; p.52 – paintbrush © musmellow/Shutterstock.com; p.52 – crayon © bsd studio/Shutterstock.com; p.53 – shapes © VasiliyArt/Shutterstock.com; p.53 – party hat © jehsomwang/Shutterstock.com; p.53 – party blower © vectorchef/Shutterstock.com; p.57 – bubble and wand © Oleksandr Panasovskyi/Shutterstock.com; p.58 – remote control © Oleksandr Panasovskyi/Shutterstock.com; p.59 – toolbox © Fresh_Studio/Shutterstock.com; p.63, 64 – heart © R Market Stock/Shutterstock.com; p.65 – children © mijatmijatovic/Shutterstock.com; p.69 – outline of child © Anna Rassadnikova/Shutterstock.com; p.70 – cushion © chempina/Shutterstock.com; p.77 – cake © suesse/Shutterstock.com; p.82 – twig © vectorisland/Shutterstock.com; p.82 – ball of string © oudiea/Shutterstock.com; p.82 – leaves © RaulAlmu/Shutterstock.com; p.82 – leaves © Red-Diamond/Shutterstock.com; p.82 – feather © Great Vector Elements/Shutterstock.com; p.86 – star © andvasiliev/Shutterstock.com; p.90 – bags of food © sokolfly/Shutterstock.com; p.91 – child relaxing © mijatmijatovic/Shutterstock.com; p.93 – water tracker © masher/Shutterstock.com; p.97 – food © Kirill Malyshev/Shutterstock.com; p.98 – banana © Hein Nouwens/Shutterstock.com; p.98 – pancakes © Martial Red/Shutterstock.com; p.99 – brain © Blamb/Shutterstock.com; p.104 – child with laptop © mijatmijatovic/Shutterstock.com; p.106 – balloon © mijatmijatovic/Shutterstock.com; p.111 – blocks © Jamila Aliyeva/Shutterstock.com; p.119 – megaphone © Keripik/Shutterstock.com; p.122 – musical notes © Vectorry/Shutterstock.com; p.129 – book © Puckung/Shutterstock.com; p.131 – gift © Artem Novosad/Shutterstock.com; p.134 – scroll © MasterGraph/Shutterstock.com; p.135 – bedroom © Aluna1/Shutterstock.com; p.136 – bunting © Neliakott/Shutterstock.com

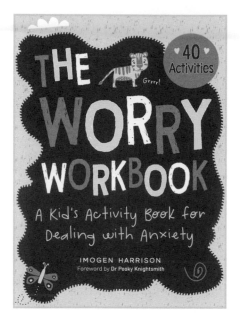

THE WORRY WORKBOOK

A Kid's Activity Book for Dealing
with Anxiety

Imogen Harrison

Paperback

ISBN: 978-1-5107-6407-1

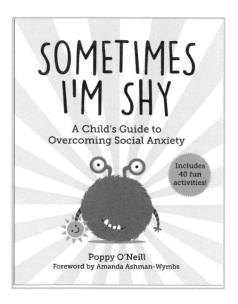

SOMETIMES I'M SHY

A Child's Guide to Overcoming
Social Anxiety

Poppy O'Neill

Paperback

ISBN: 978-1-5107-7062-1

BELIEVING IN ME
A Child's Guide to Self-Confidence
and Self-Esteem

Poppy O'Neill

Paperback

ISBN: 978-1-5107-4747-0

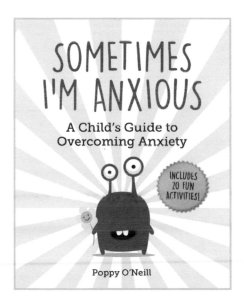

SOMETIMES I'M ANXIOUS
A Child's Guide to
Overcoming Anxiety

Poppy O'Neill

Paperback

ISBN: 978-1-5107-4748-7